CHILDREN'S GARDENS

EDWIN L. HOWARD

with a materials list newly compiled by

RICHARD L. FRANKLIN

D1471615

WESTHOLME
Yardley

Originally Published in 1940 by Studio Publications
First Westholme Paperback 2007
Westholme Edition © 2007 Westholme Publishing
Bill of Materials List © 2007 Richard L. Franklin

Published by
Westholme Publishing, LLC
Eight Harvey Avenue
Yardley, Pennsylvania 19067
www.westholmepublishing.com

ISBN 10: 1-59416-040-6
ISBN 13: 978-1-159416-040-0

First Printing
0 9 8 7 6 5 4 3 2 1

Printed in Canada on acid-free paper

CONTENTS

INTRODUCTION

It is fun to build a garden. Gardening is creative; and one of the greatest satisfactions in life is to look upon something which you, yourself, have brought into being, and to find it good.

Gardening is hard work; but every effort will show real results. You will need advice and help in creating your garden; you may have to have someone help you in preparing the soil, in building fences and shelters, and in growing the plants; but the more work you are able to do yourself, the more satisfied you will be with the result.

It is fun, too, to hunt for buried treasure; and there is a treasure hidden in your back-yard. You may have this treasure to keep as long as you live, if you who and work for it. It is neither gold nor jewels, but something far more valuable. It is health. Gardening will pay you well for all your efforts; you will have the fun of creation and the strength to enjoy fully the fruits of your labours. It is like eating your cake and having it too.

As you plan your garden you will lay out spaces for vegetables, flowers, bushes and trees; but don't forget the most important reason for the garden, which is yourself. There must be places for you, places where you can play games, places for you to dine, shady arbours for your reading, and places for you to sit and do just nothing.

The exact design of your garden will require much thought and study. You must make careful drawings on paper, and perhaps, even a model; because it is easier to change a drawing or a model, until you have a scheme that pleases you, than it is to replant and rearrange the actual paths and flowers. The first requirement of the garden plan is that it should have a definite shape. A garden which is a mass of plants is usually a mess. Its shape will be determined to a certain extent by the plot available. For instance, a square plot leads to a square pattern, or in a square plot we could make a round garden by planting out the four corners. You will plan some spot which will be the centre of interest and the paths, grass plots and flower beds will be arranged around this. The centre of interest may be a well, an open space for a picnic, a game court, or any feature which will dominate the scheme.

Remember the points of the compass and plan the tall plantings so that their shade will not blanket the lower flowers. Your climate must determine many features of the garden. In warm climates plan for shade; but in the north you will want to accent the open sunny spaces.

Flowers can be exasperating and disappointing. They refuse to bloom, or have blights and insects. So it is well to count on some additional hobby to take the place of growing plants in the garden if they should fail you. For instance, you might plan a croquet lawn, or a badminton court, a fish pool or a bird feeding station; or a picnic spot with an open grille for cooking. Such features will certainly help you to get greater pleasure from your garden.

You will want your garden to be attractive in winter, even though the hours for using it are shortened. Put in evergreens and plenty of bushes which have interestingly formed branches and seed pods. Paint the benches, or walls, or some big pots a bright colour so that they will cheer up a drab winter day. The garden which has a definite design will still interest the eye, even though the flower beds are not filled with colour.

One of the fascinating things about gardens is that they are never the same two days in succession; they are constantly changing. So do not hesitate to change your garden scheme about, as you find a better scheme. Gardens are not designed really, they are redesigned. Experience will show you that certain plants will grow better in places other than where you first set them out.

Use ideas from other gardens that you will see and enjoy, and from books and pictures. Change and adapt these ideas to your own requirements. At first keep your garden small, with only a few varieties of plants: then, as your experience grows, let it expand and become more varied. There is so much to be learned about plants at the beginning that it is wise not to rush. Above all, never become discouraged if things do not work out exactly as you had planned them at first; you are working with Mother Nature who will not always take your commands, but sometimes she will present you with an unexpected and beautiful result.

No garden is perfect; but there is not a garden in the world that has not been fun for the person who planned it, dug deep, and watched it come into being.

CHAPTER I

THE ZOO GARDEN

Are you fond of pets? Would you like to keep some rabbits, guinea pigs, or bantam chickens? An animal cage is an ideal centre of interest for a young person's garden. Around this cage would be grouped the vegetable beds in which will be grown the food for the animals.

You can have a real zoo with several kinds of pets in cages, and it will be a great success if you will be methodical in taking care of the animals. You must water and feed them regularly, and every day the cages must be cleaned. You will plan your garden to grow the food that they like.

The Bunny Garden shown here has a rabbit hutch in the centre. The entire zoo garden is placed so as to fill in the corner of a square plot, similar to the back-yard of a house. The centre of the space in front of the hutch is kept open as a play space and the vegetable plots are at the side. Two benches are placed beside the hut, a fence across the front of the garden, and the scheme is complete.

The vegetable plots will be planned carefully with plantings of the green vegetables which grow well in your locality. Lettuce and carrots, radishes and cabbages, broccoli and turnips are some of the foods to be grown. You will plant these in accordance with the directions on the packages of seeds. These directions will also tell you how far apart to space the seeds.

Of course, most animals will need other foods, besides the ones that you can grow, but your garden will furnish the larger part of their food. Rabbits, for instance, need grain as well as greens. The exact diet will be explained to you by the dealer from whom you secure your pets.

THE ZOO GARDEN

In the garden illustrated here there is only one cage shown; it is best to start with only a few animals, and then add more to your collection as you become skilled in caring for them. In this scheme, as your zoo grows, you might add two cages in place of the two benches, and then place the benches against the fence, on either side of the gate.

The hutch is not difficult to make. You can use any wood that is available, such as crate wood. The bottom of the cage has openings, so that the animal droppings can fall through and be raked up. This kind of a bottom will also dry out rapidly after it has been flushed out with the hose. The sides of the hutch are covered with poultry mesh wire and in cold weather the back and sides should be closed in with boards. The roof is made of rough boards covered with tar paper and over this is a thatch of grass.

The thatch roof can be made of straw bottle wrappers pressed flat and tacked to the boards; or it can be made by tying bunches of well-dried grass or strap. The individual pieces of thatch are laid over each other like shingles; and then trimmed neatly with garden shears. This thatch roof will keep the cage cool in the hot sun. Rabbits suffer from the heat and if you live in a very warm climate, you will need to place their cage in the shade of trees. On a very hot day it is well to put some wet burlap on the floor of the cage to keep it cool.

Don't forget to clean out the cage every day. Remove all uneaten food, clean out the water container, clean the floor. Rake up the space under the cage and put the manure on the flower beds in other parts of the garden. Do not use rabbit manure on the vegetable beds where their food is grown.

If you decide to raise guinea pigs, or bantam chickens, the cages can be similar to the rabbit cage. Do not hesitate to change the design shown here, if you can think of a better one. Or you may have pet squirrels, white mice, a raccoon, but don't start something you can't successfully take care of. Perhaps you can interest other friends in raising animals, then you can swap

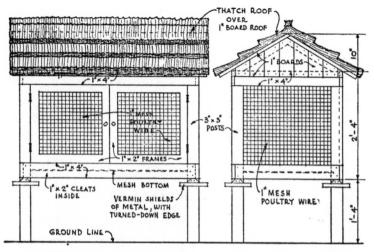

FRONT ELEVATION

THATCH ROOF OVER 1" BOARD ROOF

1" BOARDS

1" x 4"

1" MESH POULTRY WIRE

1" x 2" FRAMES

3" x 3" POSTS

10"

2'-4"

1'-4"

1" x 4"

1" x 2" CLEATS INSIDE

MESH BOTTOM

VERMIN SHIELDS OF METAL, WITH TURNED-DOWN EDGE

GROUND LINE

END ELEVATION

1" MESH POULTRY WIRE

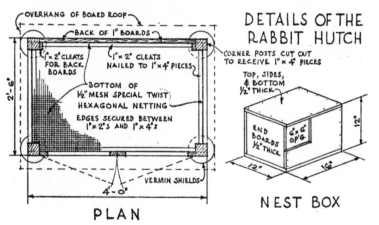

OVERHANG OF BOARD ROOF

BACK OF 1" BOARDS

1" x 2" CLEATS FOR BACK BOARDS

1" x 2" CLEATS NAILED TO 1" x 4" PIECES

BOTTOM OF ½" MESH SPECIAL TWIST HEXAGONAL NETTING

EDGES SECURED BETWEEN 1" x 2"s AND 1" x 4"s

VERMIN SHIELDS

2'-6"

4'-0"

PLAN

DETAILS OF THE RABBIT HUTCH

CORNER POSTS CUT OUT TO RECEIVE 1" x 4" PIECES

TOP, SIDES, & BOTTOM ½" THICK

END BOARDS ½" THICK

4" x 6" OP'G.

12"

12"

16"

NEST BOX

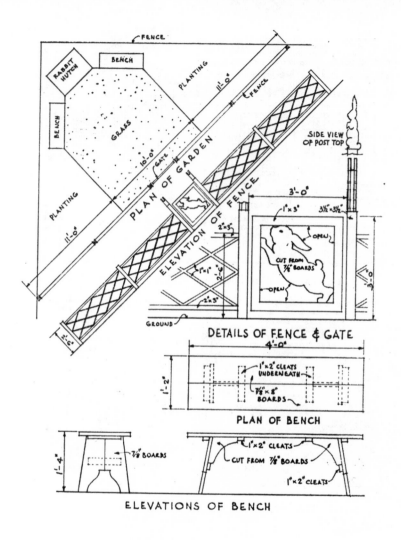

FENCE

BENCH

RABBIT HUTCH

PLANTING

11'-0"

FENCE

BENCH

GRASS

10'-0"

GATE

PLAN OF GARDEN

PLANTING

11'-0"

ELEVATION OF FENCE

2'-6"

2"x3"

1"x1"

2"x3"

GROUND

SIDE VIEW OF POST TOP

3'-0"

1"x3"

3½"x3½"

OPEN

CUT FROM ⅞" BOARDS

OPEN

3'-0"

DETAILS OF FENCE & GATE

4'-0"

1"x2" CLEATS UNDERNEATH

⅞"x8" BOARDS

1'-2"

PLAN OF BENCH

⅞" BOARDS

1'-4"

1"x2" CLEATS

CUT FROM ⅞" BOARDS

1"x2" CLEATS

ELEVATIONS OF BENCH

pets. It is often a good thing to start with one kind and then change over to another; but remember, it isn't right to keep pets if you are not willing to take care of them.

Bantam chickens are lots of fun. They do not need much space and their eggs, though tiny, taste even better than the regular hen's eggs. The chicks are very cute and the grown birds are pretty. For the chickens you will have to have space for corn and other grains in the garden and you will have to plan to store your harvest for the winter season. This means planning in advance, which is difficult if you are young. The younger we are the quicker we want results. But anything worth having is worth working and waiting for; so do not be discouraged.

A zoo will keep you busy all year round, but if you take care of it regularly it will not be too much work and it is certain to be lots of fun. The garden, which is definitely a part of it, will have a real reason for being. It is more fun to grow plants for a definite purpose, and seed time and harvest will take on a new meaning.

CHAPTER II

THE WATER GARDEN

A water garden is the easiest kind of garden to take care of. Once you have prepared it, it will take care of itself with only a little attention from you. It is most attractive on the warm days of summer and gives a sparkle to the garden that you can achieve in no other way. If you have some fish in your pool, they will keep away the mosquitoes by eating the wiggle-tails, and they are interesting to watch and study.

The simplest kind of water garden is a wash tub sunk into the earth so that the rim is level with the ground. About the edge of the pool, place flat stones so that the rim of the tub is hidden. The tub should be filled with about twelve inches of rich garden soil (water lilies like a mixture of one half cow manure and one half good earth). In this soil you plant your water lily roots and the cabomba or other under-water plants which will generate oxygen. Before you put the water in the tub, cover the surface of the earth with two inches of clean sand to keep the mud from mixing with the water. It will also keep bits of straw or wood from floating to the surface. Add the water very gently, filling the pool to the brim. Then we add the floating plants, such as water hyacinth, and the fish; and perhaps also some water snails; then the pool is finished.

The water in the pool will have to be filled up from the hose from time to time as it evaporates. It will never become stagnant if you have the proper balance of animal and vegetable life. The man from whom you secure your water plants and animals will advise you on the exact proportion.

The building of the Rose Boat is not very difficult but you will need the help of someone skilled in carpentry to build the form in which the shape

WATER GARDEN AND ROSE BOAT

of the boat is cast in concrete. The first step is digging the trench for the circular edge. Dig this trench as deep and thick as shown on the working drawing. The sides of the trench will serve as the form for the concrete. Then fill the trench with concrete; when the concrete has thoroughly hardened, about ten days in dry weather, dig out the centre of the pool and pour in the floor. Next build the boat form of wood and plyboard bent to the curves and pour the concrete in this form. When it has thoroughly set, you remove the forms and paint the sides of the boat and the bottom and sides of the pool with cement and water, mixed to the consistency of rich cream. This is the best waterproofing mixture that you can use.

Now fill the middle of the pool with rich garden soil, plant the main mast and then the roses. You may want to keep a little grass plot in the centre of the ship as a place for sitting, or you might use some other flowering plant such as petunias, to give a gay effect when the roses are not in bloom.

The gangplank is made of two boards cleated together on the under side. They can be raised and laid to one side when you do not wish to have anyone come aboard.

If you can find an old row boat which is no longer serviceable, you can substitute it for the concrete ship. This would, of course, be much simpler than the concrete. The chances are that, even though filled with earth, it would not rot away for a year or two, especially if you give it two coats of good paint, inside and out. To keep the boat from sinking you should place it on a platform of boxes filled with stones or bricks, under the water.

About the water garden you should plant those flowers which love boggy places. Siberian iris and iris versicolor, do not mind getting their feet wet; but do not use German iris, as the rhizomes from which they grow will quickly rot in the dampness. Forget-me-not will grow like a weed, as will cat-tails and arrowroot. You will have to water these very often and never let the soil about them become caked and dry.

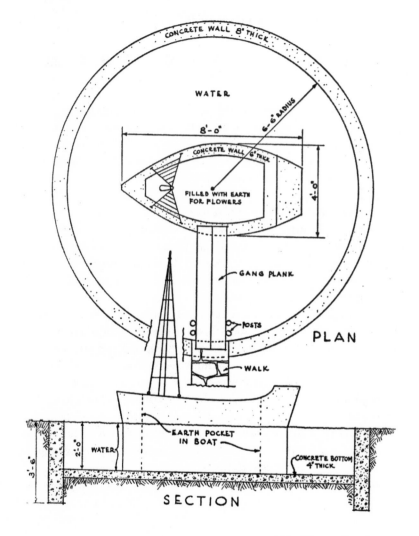

CONCRETE WALL 8" THICK

WATER

8'-0"

6'-6" RADIUS

CONCRETE WALL 6" THICK

FILLED WITH EARTH
FOR FLOWERS

4'-0"

GANG PLANK

POSTS

WALK

PLAN

EARTH POCKET
IN BOAT

WATER

2'-0"

3'-6"

CONCRETE BOTTOM
4" THICK

SECTION

CHAPTER III

THE LITTLE FARM

Do you like spinach? If you don't, then you have never had it fresh out of your own garden. Spinach, or any other vegetable, takes on a new and richer flavour when you have been responsible for its raising Another plant that will completely win you over to greens is New Zealand spinach which you can harvest late in the autumn, after the frost has taken all the other vegetables.

Every garden should have some edible plants to round out its usefulness. Try an edging of carrots about a rose bed; the foliage is like a lacy fern. One day while the carrots are still small, pull one up, wash it in cold water and eat it just so; it tastes like a very good nut. If you plan your crops carefully, you can have the thrill of feeding the whole family from your small "farm," for a number of meals.

The first requirement of a successful vegetable garden is the proper preparation of the soil. If the ground is too sandy, you must add humus; digging in peat moss or well-rotted vegetable matter are two ways of adding humus. If the soil is heavy clay, you must add sand as well as humus. The ground must be fertile, and a wheelbarrow of barnyard manure to every square yard is about right. If you cannot get manure you will have to use commercial fertilizer which contains the three necessities for plant growth, nitrogen, phosphorus and potash. The directions for applying this fertilizer are usually to be found on the package; if no directions are given, you should consult the dealer who sells it to you.

Constantly you must till the earth. In the early spring, dig deep and break up all the clods; and at all seasons, rake, hoe and cultivate. Good tools

THE LITTLE FARM

will make the work more fun; for this work you will need at least the following tools. First, you will need a spade, and a digging fork, a hoe, and a rake; and for the close work, you will need a trowel and a hand cultivator.

Always clean the tools after using them and put them away. This will save time (and the tools). Don't forget to water the garden if the soil starts to dry out. The vegetables are about ninety per cent. water so they must have moisture for growth. The garden will not have to be watered so often if the ground surface is always kept loose by cultivation. This crumbly top layer of earth will keep the sun and air from drawing up the moisture from deeper down. Never sprinkle the garden, soak it. The sprinkling wets the earth for only a few inches so that the roots grow up to reach it; then comes a dry spell and the roots are killed. Cultivate after every rain or hosing.

In the place where you keep your tools, you should have a special shelf for bug poisons. This shelf should be painted red and placed so high that the younger children cannot reach it. There are two general types of bugs that you must fight, those that chew, such as beetles; and those that suck the juice from the plant, such as aphis. The chewing bugs must be killed by putting poison on the leaves, and the others can be killed by a spray. You will also need dusts such as Bordeaux mixture for fungus blights. The best methods for using these poisons are explained on the packages, and you should always read the directions carefully.

There must never be any vacant spots in the vegetable garden: as soon as one crop is harvested, another one should be planted. The crops must be carefully planned; for instance, bush bean rows should be sown every two weeks until the middle of summer.

You should have an orchard of dwarf fruit trees. These little fellows yield a good harvest, they are easier than large trees to spray and prune, and they take a comparatively small area. In the old Roman gardens they often planted roses between the trees and grew them on festoons swung between the trunks. Roses and apples belong to the same plant family so they ought to get along together.

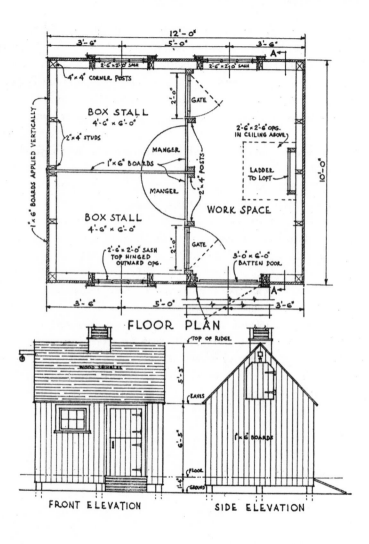

12'-0"

3'-6"   5'-0"   3'-6"

2'-6"x2'-0" SASH   2'-6"x2'-0" SASH   A

4"x4" CORNER POSTS

2'-0"

GATE

BOX STALL
4'-6" x 6'-0"

2"x4" STUDS

2'-6"x2'-6" OPG.
IN CEILING ABOVE

1"x6" BOARDS APPLIED VERTICALLY

MANGER

1"x6" BOARDS

LADDER
TO LOFT

10'-0"

MANGER

2"x4" POSTS

BOX STALL
4'-6" x 6'-0"

WORK SPACE

2'-0"

GATE

2'-6"x2'-0" SASH
TOP HINGED
OUTWARD OPG.

3'-0"x6'-0"
BATTEN DOOR

A

3'-6"   5'-0"   3'-6"

FLOOR PLAN

WOOD SHINGLES

TOP OF RIDGE

5'-3"

EAVES

1"x6" BOARDS

6'-5"

FLOOR

GROUND

FRONT ELEVATION   SIDE ELEVATION

Don't forget a berry patch, raspberries, currants and blackberries. Everbearing strawberries are easily raised in a strawberry barrel. The barrel is filled with rich earth, after a number of holes have been cut in the sides, each about four inches in diameter. The plants are placed in these holes and in the top of the barrel. If the earth seeps from the holes before the plants roots have grown sufficiently to hold it in place, stuff cheese-cloth around the plants.

A little farm is not complete without some animals. Would you like to raise some sheep? They are not difficult to take care of, if you have space for a pasture. Or would you like a goat? Billy goats sometimes smell but Nanny goats do not, and their milk is richer than a cow's. The simplest building to house them is a lean-to, which will give them some protection from the weather. The Little Barn which is drawn here is fairly expensive to build but it would provide a great deal of interest and amusement.

The Barn has two stalls (the exact size of these may have to be changed, depending upon what animals you have), also a space for the garden implements and for your indoor gardening work, such as sorting seeds and storing them. There is a loft for hay or feed, and the barn is raised on a foundation. It is easier to keep an animal stall clean and sweet if the floor can be thoroughly cleaned. Never try to raise animals unless you are going to keep them clean, feed and water them regularly and give them careful attention. They will take much time and effort but they will more than reward you.

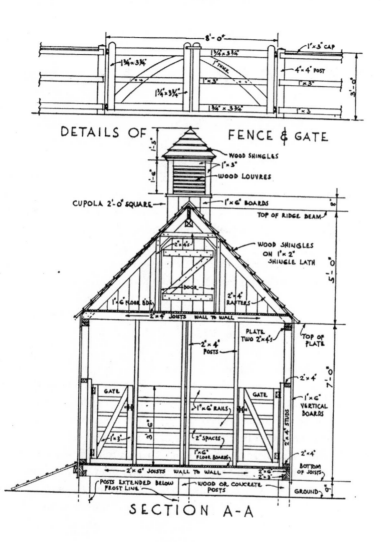

DETAILS OF   FENCE & GATE

8'-0"
1¼"×3¼"
1"THICK
1"×3"
1¼"×3¼"
1¾"×3¾"
1"×3"CAP
4"×4" POST
1"×3"
1"×3"
3'-0"

WOOD SHINGLES
1"×3"
WOOD LOUVRES
CUPOLA 2'-0" SQUARE
1"×6" BOARDS
TOP OF RIDGE BEAM
WOOD SHINGLES
ON 1"×2"
SHINGLE LATH
2"×4"s
DOOR
2"×4"
RAFTERS
1"×6" FLOOR BDS.
2"×4" JOISTS WALL TO WALL
PLATE
TWO 2"×4's
TOP OF PLATE
2"×4"
POSTS
GATE
1"×6" RAILS
2" SPACES
1"×6" FLOOR BOARDS
1"×3"
GATE
2"×4"
1"×6" VERTICAL BOARDS
2"×4" STUDS
2"×4"
BOTTOM OF JOISTS
2"×6" JOISTS WALL TO WALL
2"×6"
2"×3"
GROUND
POSTS EXTENDED BELOW FROST LINE
WOOD OR CONCRETE POSTS

SECTION A-A

CHAPTER IV

THE BIRD GARDEN

Gardens can be heard as well as seen. Haven't you ever stopped to listen to the rustle of a breeze in a thicket, the tinkle of a little fountain, or the drowsy droning of a bumble-bee? One thing I am sure you have listened for, is the first bird song of spring. Why not plan a garden that will make the birds stay with you all the year through, a little garden filled with thorny plants, to keep the bird enemies away, and berry bearing bushes and plants that have lots of seeds. There will be bird houses, a bird bath and a feeding station.

It is fascinating to watch a robin bounce over the grass, stop and cock his head on one side as though he were listening, then suddenly pull forth a long reluctant worm; then off to the nest where the wide-mouthed cheepers are waiting. The robin builds her nest on an open shelf and doesn't like a house, so you will remember to place some shelves, about five inches square, in nearby trees.

The "International Committee for Bird Preservation" has member societies in almost every country, if you get in touch with the one nearest you, that Society will gladly give you information on the birds of your locality.

In the northern climates, when the ground is covered with snow, the birds especially need your help in finding food. Hang some suet in wire baskets in the trees. Another way of attracting them is to press warm suet and nut meats into pine cones and then hang the cones from the branches.

In the Bird Garden which is drawn here, the feeding station is the centre of interest. The station has a roof to ward off the snow and rain, then a

THE BIRD GARDEN

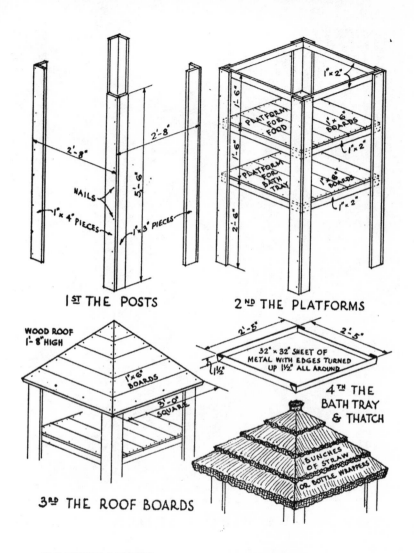

2'-8"

2'-8"

5'-6"

NAILS

1" × 4" PIECES

1" × 3" PIECES

1ST THE POSTS

1" × 2"

1'-6"

PLATFORM FOR FOOD

1" × 6" BOARDS

1'-6"

PLATFORM FOR BATH TRAY

1" × 6" BOARDS

1" × 2"

2'-6"

1" × 2"

2ND THE PLATFORMS

WOOD ROOF 1'-8" HIGH

1" × 6" BOARDS

3'-0" SQUARE

3RD THE ROOF BOARDS

2'-5"

2'-5"

32" × 32" SHEET OF METAL WITH EDGES TURNED UP 1½" ALL AROUND

1½"

4TH THE BATH TRAY & THATCH

BUNCHES OF STRAW OR BOTTLE WRAPPERS

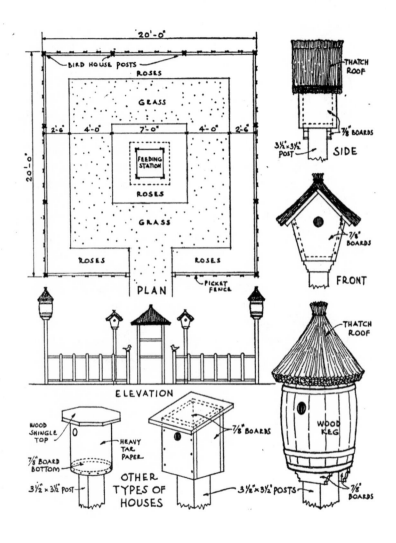

20'-0"

BIRD HOUSE POSTS

ROSES

GRASS

2'-6" 4'-0" 7'-0" 4'-0" 2'-6"

20'-0"

FEEDING STATION

ROSES

GRASS

ROSES   ROSES

PICKET FENCE

PLAN

THATCH ROOF

7/8" BOARDS

3½"×3½" POST

SIDE

7/8" BOARDS

FRONT

THATCH ROOF

WOOD KEG

7/8" BOARDS

ELEVATION

WOOD SHINGLE TOP

7/8" BOARD BOTTOM

3½"×3½" POST

HEAVY TAR PAPER

7/8" BOARDS

OTHER TYPES OF HOUSES

3½"×3½" POSTS

platform for the food, the suet, grain, and bread crumbs; beneath this is the bird bath, which is made of a sheet of metal turned up at the edges. Birds like a bath which is not over an inch and a half deep. If you have very severe winter and the feeding station is exposed to the cold winter winds, you should close in three sides of the station with rough boards. Or if you can, find some old window sashes of the right size, these could be placed so as to protect the platform.

The legs of the station rest on tin pie plates; these will keep off the field mice, or rats, which might try to climb up for the food. Around the station you will plant a climbing type rose, letting it cover the ground. It will keep the cats away with its thorns.

Climbing roses will also be on the posts that hold the bird houses, and trained across the chains which connect the posts. When you place many bird houses close together, some of them will be unoccupied, as most birds of a kind do not like to be too near each other. If you wish to attract a certain kind of bird you must build a certain kind of house, but as there is not sufficient room in this book to give all the kinds you must look up the necessary information through the local bird society.

If you live in a country with humming birds, they will visit your garden provided that you hang out small glass test tubes filled with water and a very small amount of sugar.

CHAPTER V

THE CIRCUS GARDEN

The very young cannot plant and take care of flowers, but nevertheless they should have a part of the garden devoted to them. They should have a place where they can dig and mess about in the sunshine, and if they realise that this portion of the garden is their very own, they are less liable to get into mischief in other, more cultivated, parts of the garden.

For some children it may be necessary to enclose their play space within a simple low fence, but the Circus Garden is enclosed merely with a low circular seat, the seat which forms the circus ring. The ring will be filled with sand to the depth of about two feet. If the spot is in a damp location, it is wise to have a foot of broken rock beneath the sand so that it will dry out quickly after a rainstorm. The seat is supported by the boards which are bent about stakes driven into the ground. It should be painted with bright decorations and the young proprietors of the circus should have a hand in this decoration, even though it may be a messy hand.

In the ring Mumbo-Jumbo the elephant stands patiently waiting for the ring-master to climb up over his back and slide down his trunk. He is built of boarding and his trunk is covered with smooth metal. He should be painted bright Durbar colours, perhaps an all-over tattoo design of red and blue spots on a white background. He will have to be very carefully built, so, if there is not an older member of the family who is capable, it may be necessary to call in a carpenter. If, when the elephant is all finished and in place, he is not steady on his feet, it would be wise to fasten him to stakes driven deep into the ground.

THE CIRCUS GARDEN

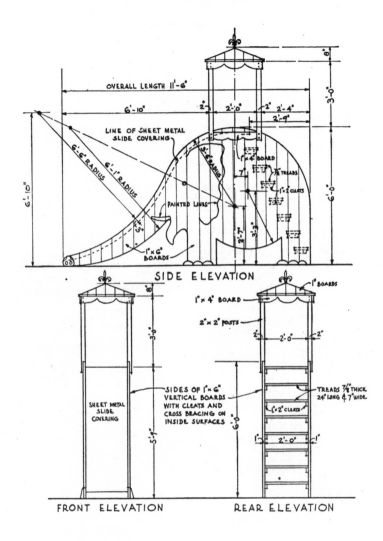

OVERALL LENGTH 11'-6"

LINE OF SHEET METAL
SLIDE COVERING

6'-10"

6'-6" RADIUS
6'-1" RADIUS

6'-10"

PAINTED LINES

1'x 4" BOARD
7/8 TREADS
1"x 2" CLEATS

1"x 6"
BOARDS

SIDE ELEVATION

8"
3'-0"
6'-0"

2" 2'-0" 2" 2'-4"
2'-9"

6" RADIUS

2'-7"
3'-3"

1" BOARDS

1"x 4" BOARD

2"x 2" POSTS

2" 2'-0" 2"

8"
3'-0"

SHEET METAL
SLIDE
COVERING

SIDES OF 1"x 6"
VERTICAL BOARDS
WITH CLEATS AND
CROSS BRACING ON
INSIDE SURFACES

TREADS 7/8" THICK
24" LONG & 7" WIDE

1"x 2" CLEATS

5'-1"

6'-0"

1" 2'-0" 1"

FRONT ELEVATION

REAR ELEVATION

The Circus Garden 33

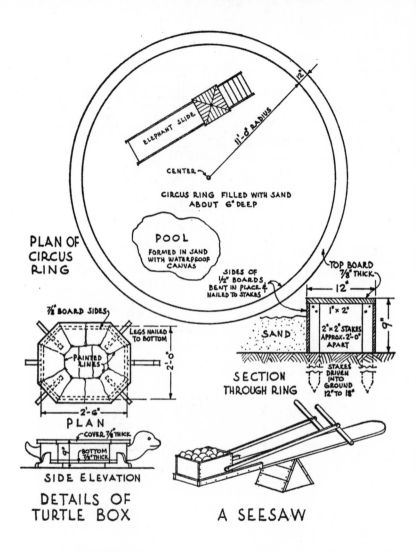

PLAN OF
CIRCUS
RING

ELEPHANT SLIDE

12"

11'-0" RADIUS

CENTER

CIRCUS RING FILLED WITH SAND
ABOUT 6" DEEP

POOL
FORMED IN SAND
WITH WATERPROOF
CANVAS

SIDES OF
1/2" BOARDS
BENT IN PLACE &
NAILED TO STAKES

TOP BOARD
7/8" THICK

12"

SAND

1" X 2"

2" X 2" STAKES
APPROX. 2'-0"
APART

9"

STAKES
DRIVEN
INTO
GROUND
12" TO 18"

SECTION
THROUGH RING

7/8" BOARD SIDES

LEGS NAILED
TO BOTTOM

PAINTED
LINES

2'-0"

2'-6"

PLAN

COVER 7/8 THICK.

BOTTOM 7/8 THICK

9"

SIDE ELEVATION

DETAILS OF
TURTLE BOX

A SEESAW

There is a Paddle-pool in the circus ring. This is very easy to make, the only thing you will need is a six-foot square of waterproof canvas. Dig a basin in the sand about a foot and one half deep and line it with the canvas, folding under and burying the corners; then fill it with water from the hose. On a very hot day it would be fun to place this pool at the end of the elephant's trunk even though a few rapid landings from the howdah atop Mumbo-Jumbo will splash out all the water.

A see-saw is very easily made and is very appropriate for the circus. On the construction page you will find a design for one that can be operated by only one sitter and gives good exercise too. If the older children are to use the ring, a strong swing and trapeze would be very useful. These should also be painted bright circus colours and the youngsters should do a large part of the painting. The grown-up should not expect too careful and neat decorations: the child will appreciate it more, if it represents his own efforts, than if it were the most exact pattern.

Sand is not the best place for a little child to play in if it is damp, and sand can hold the dew, so it is well to cover over the ring at night with canvas. A small sand box with its own cover is shown on the construction page.

Amos the turtle can be used either as a seat, or, if you hinge his shell, as a box for toys. The simplest features of the circus are the kegs which are also brilliantly painted, and are of the type in which nails are sold. The sides of some of these kegs are quite rough, so it may be necessary to give them a careful smoothing with sandpaper.

CHAPTER VI

THE TIN CAN GARDEN

If you are a city dweller and have only a backyard without good soil and sunlight, you still can have a garden. It may not be a spot filled with brightly-hued flowers but it can be a space of quiet beauty. There are always plants to be found which will grow anywhere. The ailanthus tree, for instance, while it may not appeal to you as much as a dogwood tree or a rose bush, still it has a charm of its own. I have seen it flourishing in poor city soil with little light and air.

Let us plan a little city garden in a backyard twenty feet square, hemmed in by tall buildings. First the ground. How shall we treat it? Such a space as this is often covered with a concrete pavement, which has the advantage of being easily kept clean and neat. However it is hard on the eye, holds the heat of the day, and is generally unattractive. Let us smooth out the earth of the yard and cover it with a truck layer of gravel. The gravel will allow the soot and grime to sift through and is easily freshened up with the hose.

If we would like to have a patterned floor, we could lay out a design in bricks and then fill in between them with gravel. And if we can readily locate several kinds of gravel we might put alternate squares of the various colours. The possibilities of pattern are many. The French, in their beautiful parterre garden designs, often use earths of several colours instead of plants.

The walls about the garden should be painted a restful colour. A pale blue or a soft yellow would be attractive. This will not be expensive if you use one of the water-colour paints which are made with a casene base. This

THE TIN CAN GARDEN

paint will not last very long out of doors but it will be good for one season at least. It is easy to apply and is put on like whitewash in one coat.

At the corners of the back wall, let us build two large brick bins to be filled with earth for the ailanthus trees, and between them a long brick seat.

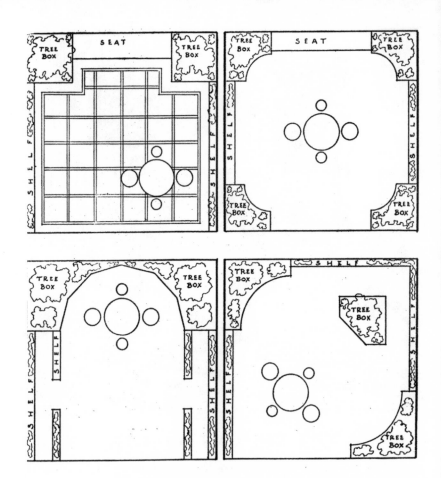

ALTERNATE PLANS FOR
A CITY GARDEN

The bins could be built of wood, if you cannot arrange to have brick; but the wood will rot away after several seasons and have to be renewed.

And now for the tin cans. Arrange these containers behind the seat to form a design. They will be painted with one coat of quick-drying lacquer, such as you can purchase at Woolworth's or similar stores. The colour will depend upon the colour of the wall. If your wall is a pale yellow it would be good to have the containers a pale blue, or a pale green. Some of the containers might be a brilliant colour to add gaiety to the scheme. The wall vases should be planted with hanging vines such as ivy or philodendron.

Along the side walls can be placed long board shelves for more plants in cans. These cans need not have holes if you put a layer of charcoal and gravel in the bottom, and do not water them so much that they become waterlogged.

The barrel chairs and the barrel table, with a board top, will complete the picture. They are not difficult to construct. The seats of the chairs can be of oilcloth stuffed with wood shavings. The furniture should be painted to carry out your general colour scheme. The paler colours are apt to make your space seem larger. If the garden faces north, an arrangement of yellow will make it appear sunny. If it is a warm place, a design which used blues will make it seem cooler.

CHAPTER VII

THE GAMES GARDEN

The garden design that you finally decide upon will almost certainly have open spaces of lawn to contrast with the flower beds and foliage borders. Why not make these lawns the proper size for games? The real gardener has little time for play because his time is so much occupied with the plants; but the visitor must be given something to do so that he will not be in the way. Games will greatly increase the fun in the garden.

On the page of diagrams you will find the standard sizes for a number of outdoor games. If a lack of space makes it necessary, you can reduce the standard size, in proportion, to suit your requirements. However, the full size courts are much to be preferred, even for younger people.

Lawn-tennis is the most popular game for the garden but the court requires much space and constant care. A fine turf is the perfect floor but is often difficult to keep in shape, so you may have to plan on clay, or one of the various patent materials, for the court. The enclosure, which should be ten feet high, can also be built in a number of ways; cedar posts with poultry mesh wire stretched between, is one of the least expensive. On this you will plant vines, such as clematis or honeysuckle; avoid roses as the thorns are not pleasant to back into by mistake while reaching for a ball. Consult your local sporting goods dealer for the exact kind of equipment such as the net and lines.

Handball is a fast game which will give you some fine exercise. Perhaps in your garden there is a large bare wall which you can use. Even though this wall is not as large as the standard dimension, still you can make up a game, with changes in the size of court, which will be very popular. The

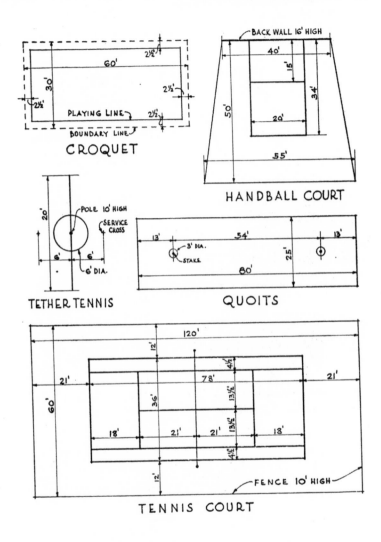

CROQUET

60'
30'
2½'
2½'
2½'
2½'
PLAYING LINE
BOUNDARY LINE

HANDBALL COURT

BACK WALL 16' HIGH
40'
15'
50'
20'
34'
55'

TETHER TENNIS

20'
POLE 10' HIGH
SERVICE CROSS
6'
6'
6' DIA.

QUOITS

13'
54'
13'
3' DIA.
STAKE
25'
80'

TENNIS COURT

120'
12'
4½'
78'
21'
21'
60'
3'6"
13½'
13½'
18'
21'
21'
13'
4½'
12'
FENCE 10' HIGH

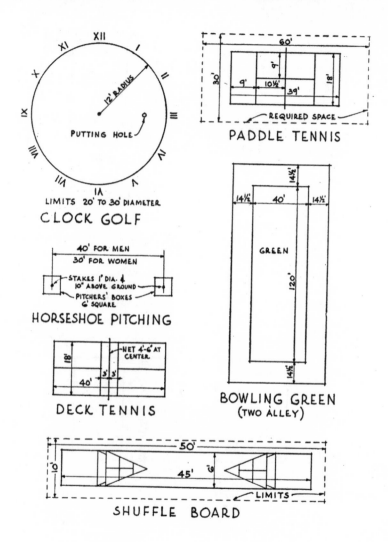

CLOCK GOLF

XII, XI, X, IX, VIII, VII, VI, V, IV, III, II, I

12' RADIUS

PUTTING HOLE

LIMITS 20' TO 30' DIAMETER

PADDLE TENNIS

60'
30'
9'
9'
10½'
39'
18'
REQUIRED SPACE

HORSESHOE PITCHING

40' FOR MEN
30' FOR WOMEN

STAKES 1" DIA. &
10" ABOVE GROUND

PITCHERS' BOXES
6' SQUARE

DECK TENNIS

18'
40'
3' 3'
NET 4'-6" AT CENTER.

BOWLING GREEN
(TWO ALLEY)

14½'
40'
14½'
14½'
GREEN
120'
14½'

SHUFFLE BOARD

50'
10'
45'
6'
LIMITS

floor of the court could be cement. If you wish a coloured cement it is very easily secured by adding colour powder to the concrete when it is mixed. The colours to use are the earth colours, browns and buffs; other colours have a tendency to fade. The exact mixture to use should be secured from your local dealer.

Tether tennis is a fine game to play to perfect your tennis stroke, and it can be played in a comparatively small area.

Badminton and deck tennis can be played on any level sward that is sufficiently large, and they can be shifted about as one place becomes worn. Paddle tennis is played on a wooden platform and is a great game for winter, spring and autumn when the ground may be difficult to play on. Paddle tennis should also have an enclosure similar to the one for tennis. Shuffleboard also requires a wooden platform and if you are planning a paddle tennis platform, part of it could be marked off for shuffleboard. The exact marking of the court you will secure from the place where you purchase the equipment.

A bowling green is a very beautiful feature in a garden, but it demands a perfect greensward. The easiest games to install are quoits and horseshoe pitching. The location of the stakes can be changed from time to time as the grass wears down.

A miniature golf course is fun to design; the arrangement could be worked out to fit the conditions of your plot, with bunkers and sand traps and water holes. It is amusing to have some silly hazards, such as driving through a barrel or over a little bridge. Clock golf is good for putting practice and here again you must have a perfect green.

The oblong shape of a croquet court is a very pleasant open centre for a bordered garden. The boundaries might be marked with a six-inch wide board which will serve as an edging for the flower beds, the beds would be raised to the top of the boards.

So plan your space to include one or more games that the entire family can enjoy, surround the courts with well thought out plantings, and you will find that your garden will become the centre of interest in the neighbourhood.

CHAPTER VIII

THE FOREST GARDEN

If you are fortunate enough to have a wooded spot to develop as your garden, you can create a fascinating place to grow wild plants and native flowers. This kind of a garden is in some ways more difficult and in others easier than the usual open sunny garden. It is easier to take care of because you will encourage the plants to grow as they wish without too much trimming and arranging. It is more difficult because you must have a scheme which will be carefully planned without appearing to be planned.

You will have to study carefully some untouched spots of woodland and observe how the native plants like to grow. Jonquils, for instance, like to be in drifts; not planted in regular rows. Some plants like to be among rocks, while others like a low damp location. Each one has its own preferences for the amount of sunlight and its relation to other plants. You must arrange your space so that each type of flower has a suitable setting and yet does not look as though it had been arranged.

If you plan to fence-in the space, a very natural looking fence can be made by nailing saplings and branches to boards, the boards should be nailed to posts set about every five feet. Over this you can grow vines such as Virginia creeper which is a woodland vine, but many of the vines with good flowers, such as morning glory, will not bloom well in the shade.

Your space should be planned with paths and little clearings. The paths can be kept clear by watering them with salt water. Mix the water with ice cream salt, about two cups full to a gallon of water. Be careful in using it and remember to clean the sprinkler after use before watering any flowers.

THE FOREST GARDEN

If the ground has a tendency to be muddy, you might cover the paths with sand and gravel, peat moss, or tanbark.

The paths should lead to some definite spot, such as a clearing, a great rock or tree, or a rustic bench. When the path has led you to that object, there should be other paths leading you further. It is fun to wander through a woodland without retracing your steps or coming to a dead end.

Just which plants to grow will depend upon your climate and the local flowers available.

An ideal shelter for the woodland garden would be an American Indian teepee. In the Sioux language tee (pronounced tea) means "dwelling," the word pee means "used for;" so teepee means "used for a dwelling." This is a better word than wigwam which means a shelter and could refer to the huts of bark in which the Indians of Eastern America lived except when they were travelling, at which times they used teepees.

The Indian teepees were quite large, the poles about twenty-five feet long, and inside there was space for three or four beds. The beds were placed about the small hearth in the centre, but the teepee sketched here is smaller. There were two smoke flaps at the top to let out the smoke, and they could be closed in bad weather. The dwellings of the Indians of the great Western plains were made of buffalo hides, before the Pale-face brought canvas. These teepees took from fifteen to twenty hides to cover them.

If you would like to have a wigwam instead of the teepee, you can design one yourself. You would stick saplings about a foot deep into the ground, in two rows about five feet apart. Then you would bend the rows of saplings together and tie them to form a round arch. Next fasten cross pieces of light wood to make cross members; and finally cover the frame with canvas or branches.

Another type of a house for the forest is a Jungle Tree House. This will be a platform of boards braced in the branches of a big tree, with a board or

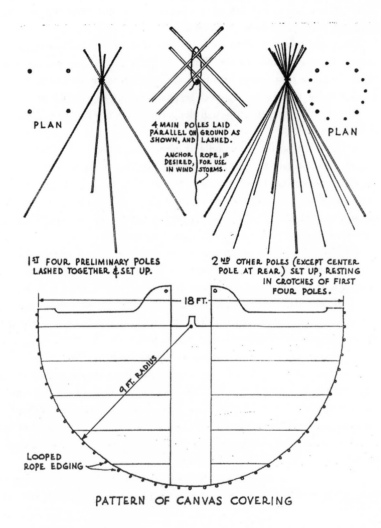

PLAN

4 MAIN POLES LAID
PARALLEL ON GROUND AS
SHOWN, AND LASHED.

ANCHOR ROPE, IF
DESIRED, FOR USE
IN WIND STORMS.

PLAN

1ST FOUR PRELIMINARY POLES
LASHED TOGETHER & SET UP.

2ND OTHER POLES (EXCEPT CENTER
POLE AT REAR) SET UP, RESTING
IN CROTCHES OF FIRST
FOUR POLES.

18 FT.

9 FT. RADIUS

LOOPED
ROPE EDGING

PATTERN OF CANVAS COVERING

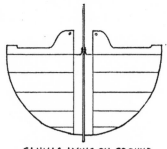

CANVAS LYING ON GROUND
WITH POLE ATTACHED

3RD. CANVAS LAID ON GROUND WITH
INSIDE UP. CENTER REAR POLE
LAID ON CANVAS, AND SMALL
FLAP AT SMOKE HOLE TIED TO
POLE AT POINT WHERE POLE WILL
INTERSECT OTHER POLES.

4TH. POLE SET UP IN ITS PLACE AT
REAR, CANVAS DRAWN AROUND
OTHER POLES AND PINNED UP
THE FRONT WITH WOODEN PINS.

5TH. POLES PUSHED OUT AND
ADJUSTED FROM INSIDE, TO
TIGHTEN CANVAS COVERING.

6TH. COVERING FASTENED TO
GROUND WITH PEGS OR SMALL
STAKES THROUGH LOOPS IN ROPE
EDGING.

7TH. TIPS OF LAST TWO POLES
INSERTED IN HOLES OR POCKETS
OF SMOKE-HOLE FLAPS, AND
POLES SET IN PLACE,
HOLDING SMOKE-HOLE
FLAPS OPEN.

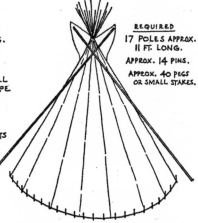

REQUIRED

17 POLES APPROX.
11 FT. LONG.

APPROX. 14 PINS.

APPROX. 40 PEGS
OR SMALL STAKES.

REAR VIEW OF TEEPEE
SHOWING LAST TWO POLES IN PLACE.

DOOR

8TH. DOOR OPENING CUT IN CANVAS (TO FIT DOOR),
EDGE OF OPENING BOUND, AND DOOR (OF CANVAS
COVERING ON OVAL FRAME OF BENT SAPLINGS) SET
IN PLACE AND TIED SO THAT IT SWINGS OPEN
AND CLOSED.

The Forest Garden 49

canvas roof. The exact design you yourself will have to determine as the house must fit the tree and no two trees are alike. This is the kind of a house Tarzan would build.

The shelter, whichever kind you decide to have, will add much to the joy of living in the forest. It will give a centre about which you will arrange the clearings, the paths and the groups of plantings.

CHAPTER IX

THE PICNIC GARDEN

For the all-round enjoyment of your garden in which you will work and play, it is good to include a space where you can cook and eat. Even though you may be able to grow the tenderest lettuce and the crispest radishes in the neighbourhood, you still haven't completed the usefulness of the garden until you have dined on the garden produce out in the open.

The first requirement of the picnic spot is a comfortable table and seats. You will find the working drawing for a table with benches on the page of diagrams. This is the table which has been used so extensively in public camping grounds. If your outdoor dining-room is in a wooded spot you might stain the woodwork a brown or grey; if it is in a flowery place, you could repeat the flower colours in the table, and use a green oil cloth cover for the top and edges of the boards.

The dining space might be a gravel covered clearing, if you have difficulty growing strong turf. The gravel space can easily be kept neat and you can keep the weeds away by sprinkling it from time to time with salt water, a cup full of coarse salt to a gallon of water.

The next most important feature is a place for cooking. It is easier to prepare the food in the house but it is more fun to do it outside. The actual fire for cooking can be very small, a big fire is a nuisance; it is hot to work over and the smoke gets in your eyes. A small bed of hot coals is perfect for the few pots or the grille. Charcoal gives the hottest fire and in the open we shall need a very hot fire as so much of the heat is lost. To start your cooking experiments you might build your fire on a small paved place, -with paving of either bricks or stones. For the first luncheon you could plan the following; bacon, crisped over the coals on long green sticks; toasted rolls and butter; a salad of mixed greens from the garden; and for dessert, candied apples. Bury the apples in the hot coals until their skins crack, take them out and wipe them off and roll them in brown sugar, hold them on long sticks over the fire until the sugar melts.

If you plan to roast meats, it is best to have some form of grille. An easy one consists of two low platforms on either side of the fire, across this several iron pipes on which rests a metal doormat. The doormat makes a fine " stone " top, either for pots or for directly grilling the meats. If the mat is of new galvanised metal you must heat it up well to drive off any fumes from the metal before placing meat upon it.

The next step in fireplace building is to have a flue to draw away the smoke; such a scheme is the one shown in the working drawing. Some meats, such as beef, are tenderest if they are cooked very fast. For this you will make two baskets to hold charcoal and hang the steaks in a grille between them. The heat from both sides, at once, will drive the juices of the meat to the centre and it will not dry out as readily as if you cooked only one side at a time. The perfect steak is well peppered with freshly ground pepper and rubbed with a clove or garlic; it is then seared until a black crust is formed. This is done by pressing the two baskets dose to the grille, then push the baskets back a little to cook the meat through. Just before carving the meat it should be well salted and buttered.

If you should want an icebox to keep drinks cool, it is not difficult to make one which will be satisfactory. It will consist of one box inside another with a hinged cover. The space between the boxes should be at least four inches and stuffed with crumpled newspapers or sawdust. The inner box must be made watertight, either with a metal lining, or roofing paper and tar. There should be a small pipe to drain the water from the bottom. The insulating material will not be efficient if it gets wet.

THE PICNIC GARDEN

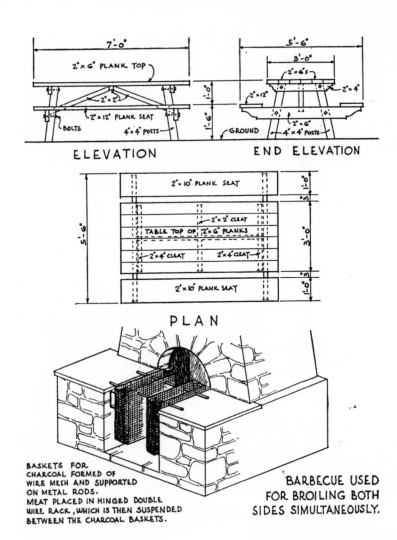

7'-0"

2" x 6" PLANK TOP

2" x 2"

2" x 12" PLANK SEAT

BOLTS

4" x 4" POSTS

ELEVATION

5'-6"

3'-0"

2" x 6"s

2" x 4"

2" x 12"

2" x 6"

4" x 4" POSTS

GROUND

1'-0"

1'-6"

END ELEVATION

2" x 10" PLANK SEAT

2" x 2" CLEAT

TABLE TOP OF 12" x 6" PLANKS

2" x 4" CLEAT   2" x 4" CLEAT

2" x 10" PLANK SEAT

5'-6"

1'-0"

3"

3'-0"

3"

1'-0"

PLAN

BASKETS FOR
CHARCOAL FORMED OF
WIRE MESH AND SUPPORTED
ON METAL RODS.
MEAT PLACED IN HINGED DOUBLE
WIRE RACK, WHICH IS THEN SUSPENDED
BETWEEN THE CHARCOAL BASKETS.

BARBECUE USED
FOR BROILING BOTH
SIDES SIMULTANEOUSLY.

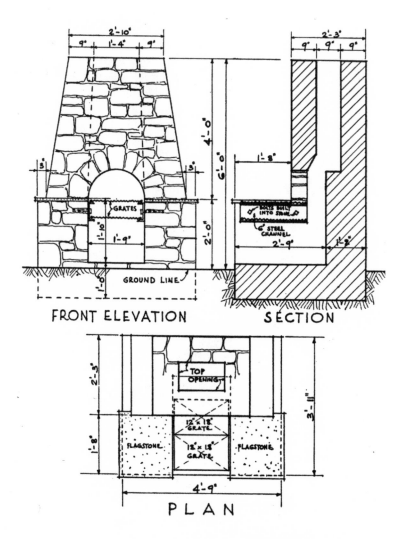

2'-10"

9" 1'-4" 9"

4'-0"

6'-9"

3"

GRATES

3"

1'-6"

1'-9"

2'-0"

1'-0"

GROUND LINE

FRONT ELEVATION

2'-3"

9" 9" 9"

1'-8"

BOLTS BUILT INTO STONE

6" STEEL CHANNEL

2'-9"

1'-2"

SECTION

2'-3"

TOP OPENING

3'-11"

1'-8"

FLAGSTONE

12" x 12" GRATE

12" x 12" GRATE

FLAGSTONE

4'-9"

PLAN

The chief advantage of having an outdoor dining-room is that it is always ready and you will dine out more often if the work is made easy. It can be so arranged that it is a central feature of the garden around which you group the flower and vegetable beds in a design. It is much easier to make a design, once you have decided on a central feature.

CHAPTER X

W I N D O W   G A R D E N S
O U T S I D E

There is often not sufficient space available for the young person to have a garden of his own, but there is one kind of garden which takes almost no space at all—the window box. All you need is a sunny window and a little patience.

Flowers will bloom readily in the sun; but it is not absolutely necessary that the window has a southern exposure. A northern window can be very attractive but in this case it is wise to plan for just a green foliage effect.

You will have to design your own boxes to fit your own window, but, whatever your design, the first requirement is that it must be fastened securely. Use screws to fix it in place, in preference to nails, for it must be secure against wind storms and heavy rains.

Over a doorway, you will want a box that will not leak. This can be ensured by lining it with a heavy sheet of roofing paper, carefully folded at the corners so that there is no break. Or you could use a sheet of metal, either with the corners folded or soldered. Plants will grow just as well in a container that has no hole in the bottom as in one with a hole, but you must put a layer of charcoal in the bottom to keep the soil sweet and change the soil each season.

You can make a box of several different levels to make it more interesting than just a plain box; a kind of step design. The flowers can be kept in their pots and the pots placed in the steps; or the steps can be filled with earth and the flowers transplanted. If you plan to use pots, it is well to clean them thoroughly and give them two coats of good lead and oil paint. This will keep the earth from drying out too fast.

A semi-circular base, braced by a bracket of some ornamental form, with an edging cut out of sheet metal, would give you a good beginning for a flower box. A high metal edging is ideal to keep pots from being blown over in the wind. It would be fine to cut this edging from sheet copper, copper which weighs 16 ounces per square foot. The copper can be made to turn that wonderful blue green colour by scrubbing it with vinegar and salt, then allowing it to soak in the solution for a day or so. It may not take on a good colour until it has been in place on the window sill for a while, however. Remember to remove all traces of the salt from the inside surface, as it might damage the plants if you are planting them in a soil filled container, rather than pots.

If your windows are casements and open out, they may knock the tops off any flowers which are grown below them. You can therefore arrange shelves down the sides for such a type of window. The shelves are triangular and screwed to the wall behind them, or it may be easier to put a strip of wood under them and let the long edge rest on that. The points of the triangles are held in place by a length of rope which is knotted just below the point and fastened to the wall two feet or so above the top shelf. A thin strip of metal is wrapped around the rope and fastened to each shelf. To be sure that the pots will not fall off, you might cut circular holes to receive them. In many cases it is not possible to fasten into the walls, as, for instance, when they are of stone. You will then have to employ some method of fixing to the window frame. You can fix your window box to two supports fastened to the sill. Two chains, or stout ropes, will hold up the ends of the supports. Your shelf can have holes cut to receive the pots. These holes could be so large that the pots go almost all the way through and rest on their rims, or

WINDOW GARDENS

alternatively only an inch or so, according to the size of hole. Don't forget to have some vines to twine up the chains.

Now think over all the designs and select the features that will best answer your problem, then make some boxes that are different and better than any others that have been made!

CHAPTER XI

WINDOW GARDENS INSIDE

As the summer days become shorter and frost threatens, you could have fun in planning to move a small part of your garden indoors. At every window that is available you can have a window garden, a bit of summer that will be with you all winter.

For real flowers you will have to have a sunny window, but even the north window can be enlivened by a frame of green. Some of the flowers will not stand the transplanting to indoors but many of them, such as geraniums and petunias, will thrive. In transplanting them you will cut back the branches by about half because most of the summer growth will die back. You will want some grape ivy and some philodendron, two vines that will grow anywhere, to fill out your scheme.

The pots, or boxes, should be watered regularly but be careful not to drown them, just enough to keep the earth moist. Be sure to arrange the pots in saucers so that the excess water will not spill on the floor. If you are using boxes with holes in the bottom, place them over pie tins. It is not necessary to have holes in the containers if you have a layer of pebbles and charcoal at the bottom.

You can have a vine curtain which springs from a plain box mounted on legs. If you have a table, this could be used and the box made to fit it. The plants are placed in the box in saucered pots, or the box could be lined with metal and then filled with earth and flowers. The curtains are made by running heavy cord up over three wooden brackets at the head of the window.

A DRUM GARDEN

The metal shelf brackets that you can buy at Woolworth's could be used instead of the wooden ones, if you wish. The box and its supporting legs and the brackets should be painted green to serve as a background for the vines.

You could make a lattice for your vines which would be made of green twine stretched between screw-eyes. In the base it would be useful to have three drawers for your gardening supplies and tools. These could, however, be omitted if you wish to simplify the design. You might substitute a border of painted flowers. I would not use bright colours though, if you have flowering plants in the box, as artificial colours are apt to conflict with the real colours, but you would be safe with a fairly wide choice of shades of green.

The easiest window garden possible consists of a number of tin cans nailed to the woodwork. If you do not wish to have too many holes made in the window trim, nail the tins to a piece of board and then fasten up the board with screws at either end. Across the bottom you could use the larger size tins than the ones up the sides and across the top. All the tins could be painted a pale colour to go with the colour scheme of your room. One coat of lacquer, after you have soaked off all traces of the paper labels, will be enough. If the containers are to hold only greenery, you might decorate them with some gay peasant designs.

Again, you could make a drum garden. It is not difficult and would be especially appropriate for a boy's room. First make two flat semi-circles of wooden boards, fastened together with cleats on the inner surfaces. Then, along the edges of these, nail the side, bending it to the curve; the side could be of heavy cardboard, or thin plyboard. Third, two narrow strips of wood are nailed to the edges and in these are placed screweyes. Finally, clothes line is laced between the screweyes. The top of the drum would look well if covered with white oil cloth and it would be easy to keep clean. The oil cloth, if you decide to use it, should be stretched over the top before the side is nailed on.

These window gardens are fascinating to arrange. How would you like to make a model of your outdoor garden on the top of the drum?

For this you will need a metal tray, the shape of the drum top; the tray should have an edge turned up at the sides six inches deep. In this you will place the earth and rocks and the dish-pan pool, and arrange the flowers and vines about them. If you would like some little houses and figures, you can easily cut them out of soap with a penknife. Paint them with water-colours and give them a coat of collodion, which you can get from a chemist or drug store. These will last for several months and will give the garden a great appearance of reality. Be careful to use plants with small leaves so that they will not too greatly dwarf the figures. If you plan carefully you will have a garden that friends from all around will crowd in to see.

CHAPTER XII

THE ENCHANTED
FLOWER GARDEN

In gardening we must be prepared for many disappointments. Mother Nature is a changeable lady, and often plants and flowers do not do as well as we had hoped they would. In order to conceal the shortcomings of one feature of the garden, it is well to have other, features to take up the interest. For instance, the beautiful shape of a flower bed will comfort us if the flowers themselves are not doing well.

This garden, in addition to having an interesting shape, has three features which do not depend upon flowers; the fence, the wishing-well, and the Hansel and Gretel playhouse. These features will give it colour and sentimental appeal even when there are no flowers.

The fence is made of cut out boards and can be painted bright colours, or you can use the brown colour scheme of gingerbread men. The eyes and mouths of the men can be either painted on, or cut out.

The wishing-well is really a small water garden and consists of a wash tub, raised on a platform of wood or masonry, and surrounded by a framework of wood, covered with metal lath and stucco. If you have some old bricks, or some medium-sized stones, the outside of the well could be built up of these. It will have to be refilled from the hose from time to time and should also be stocked with fish and under-water plants to keep the water dear: as well as some flowering water plants.

The playhouse can be built of old boards and stained and painted. The outside could, alternatively, be built of the kind of wall board which your

THE ENCHANTED FLOWER GARDEN

local lumber dealer recommends. The edges, around the door and at the corners of the house, can be cut from separate pieces of wood to resemble cakes and cookies. The main part of the walls should be painted white. The white

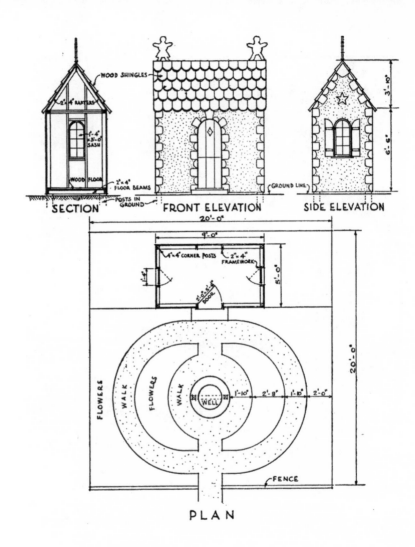

WOOD SHINGLES

2"x 4" RAFTERS

1'-4"
3'-0"
SASH

WOOD FLOOR

2"x 4"
FLOOR BEAMS

POSTS IN
GROUND

SECTION

3'- 10"

6'- 6"

FRONT ELEVATION

SIDE ELEVATION

GROUND LINE

20'- 0"

9'- 0"

4"x 4" CORNER POSTS

2"x 4"
FRAMEWORK

5'- 0"

2'-0"x 5'-2"
DOOR

20'- 0"

FLOWERS

WALK

FLOWERS

WALK

WELL

1'-10"   2'- 8"   1'- 8"   2'- 0"

FENCE

PLAN

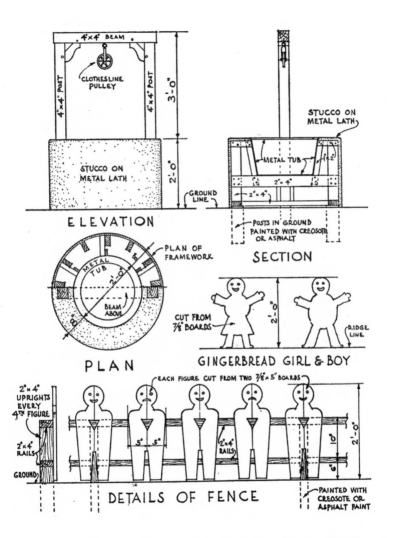

4"×4" BEAM

CLOTHESLINE PULLEY

4"×4" POST

4"×4" POST

3'-0"

STUCCO ON METAL LATH

2'-0"

GROUND LINE

ELEVATION

STUCCO ON METAL LATH

METAL TUB

1'-2"

2"×4"

2"×4"

POSTS IN GROUND PAINTED WITH CREOSOTE OR ASPHALT

SECTION

PLAN OF FRAMEWORK

METAL TUB

2'-0"

8"

8"

BEAM ABOVE

PLAN

CUT FROM 7/8" BOARDS

2'-0"

RIDGE LINE

GINGERBREAD GIRL & BOY

EACH FIGURE CUT FROM TWO 7/8"×5" BOARDS

2"×4" UPRIGHTS EVERY 4TH FIGURE

2"×4" RAILS

5" 5"

2"×4" RAILS

10"

2'-0"

6"

GROUND

PAINTED WITH CREOSOTE OR ASPHALT PAINT

DETAILS OF FENCE

paint will resemble icing if you add white sand, or marble dust, to the paint. The round ends of the roof shingles can be cut with a sharp knife and can be stained but not painted, as painted shingles are very apt to curl and warp. I would like to tell you exactly which flowers are the easiest and quickest to grow in your garden, but these flowers vary so greatly in different parts of the world that what is true of one locality is different in another. The beds around the wishing well I would plant with low flowers. Perhaps you could edge the beds with dwarf ageratum and fill the centres with petunias. The colours of the petunias can be mixed, or you could use all blue, all white, or all pink; the beds outlined with the pale blue of the ageratum and filled with pink would be very pretty. For the early spring these beds could be filled with pink tulips and around the edge a row of blue scillas and grape hyacinths.

On practically all packages of seeds you will find exact directions for planting them. Follow these and also ask advice from other gardeners in your neighbourhood. I have never found a person interested in gardens who would not gladly share the results of his experience with the beginner. The man from whom you buy your seeds or plants wants you to be successful and will help you all he can.

In the corner beds, I would plant low flowers at the edge; such as sweet alyssum, candytuft, portulaca; then behind them the flowers of medium height such as cornflowers, iris, cosmos and balsam; and at the back the taller flowers such as phlox, lupins, tall zinnias, hollyhocks and sun flowers.

There are two things that are necessary to remember if you want lots of flowers. First, the ground must be properly prepared before they are planted. Look up the preparation and fertilisation of the earth in your local library; there are many books on the subject. Second, you must cultivate the ground constantly. If you will stir the surface of the ground in all the flower beds after every rainfall you will not have to do any watering, except for very young plants and seedlings.

You must remember to pull up all weeds; and the proper definition of a weed is, a plant growing in a place where you do not wish it to grow.

BILLS OF MATERIALS FOR PROJECTS

Note: These lists do not include fastenings or hardware as these materials are best chosen by the builder.

1. The Zoo Garden Hutch

Item	Number	Size/Description
Corner posts	4	3″ x 3″ x 3′8″ long
Front and back stretchers	4	1″ x 4″ x 4′0″ long
Side stretchers	4	1″ x 4″ x 2′4.5″ long
Cleats for mesh bottom	2	1″ x 2″ x 3′6″ long
	2	1″ x 2″ x 2′3″ long
Back board (1/2″ plywood)	1	3′6″ x 1′10″ long
Cleats for back board	2	1″ x 2″ x 1′10″ long
Door frames	4	1″ x 2″ x 1′9″ long
	4	1″ x 2″ x 1′5″ long
End gable boards (1/2″ plywood)	2	2′ x 6″ long x 10″ at peak (2″ rise at ends and ca. 17.5″ length of slopes. Overlap top stretchers 1.5″)
Roof boards (1/2″ plywood)	1	4′4″ x 1′9″
	1	4′4″ x 1′10″ (overlap other roof board at ridge)
Tar paper,	1	4′5″ x 3′9″
thatch,		As needed
or asphalt shingles		1/2 pack
Chicken wire for ends	2	2′2″ x 2′0″

Chicken wire for doors	2	1′7″ x 1′6″
Heavy rat wire for bottom	1	4′0″ x 2′6″
Aluminum flashing- vermin shields	4	8″ circles with centers cut out to fit corner posts

2. THE WATER GARDEN

Item	Number	Size/Description
Form for boat	5 sheets	1/4″ or 3/8″ plywood
Bracing	as needed	2″ x 4″s and 1″ x 2″s
Circular wall	2.8 cu. yds	concrete
Bottom	.5 cu. yds	concrete
Boat	.7 cu. yds	concrete
Mast	1	10′ tapered pole
4 Shrouds; 12 ratlines		from 50′ polypropylene cord
Gang plank	2	2″ x 8″ x 5.5′ long
Cleats	3	1″ x 2″ x 1′3″ long

3. THE LITTLE FARM

Item	Number	Size/Description
Foundation posts	9	4″ x 4″ x 4′0″ pressure treated
Floor boxing	2	2″ x 6″ x 11′9″ long
	2	2″ x 6″ x 10′0″ long
Floor joists	10	2″ x 6″ x 9′9″ long
Joist cleats	2	2″ x 3″ x 11′9″ long
Floor	3 3/4	4′ x 8′ sheets, 3/4″ plywood (pressure treated)
Floor plates	2	2″ x 4″ x 12′0″ long
	2	2″ x 4″ x 9′9″ long
Corner posts	4	4″ x 4″ x 6′1 1/4″ long
Front and back wall studs	8	2″ x 4″ x 6′1 1/4″ long
Side wall studs	7	2″ x 4″ x 6′4 1/4″ long

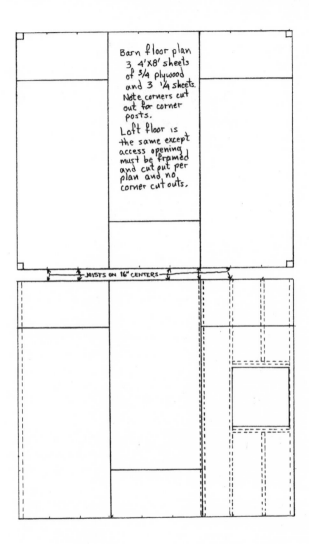

Barn floor plan
3 4'x8' sheets
of 3/4 plywood
and 3 1/4 sheets.
Note corners cut
out for corner
posts.

Loft floor is
the same except
access opening
must be framed
and cut put per
plan and no
corner cut outs.

JOISTS ON 16" CENTERS

Inside posts	6	2" x 4" x 6'5 3/4" long
Side wall top plates	4	2" x 4" x 10'0" long
Ceiling joists	10	2" x 4" x 10'0" long
Headers for ceiling opening	4	2" x 4" x 2'5 3/4" long
Loft floor	3 3/4	4' x 8' sheets, 1/2" plywood
Rafters	20	2" x 4" x 7'0" long
Ridge beam	1	2" x 6" x 12'0" long
Beam for pulley	1	4" x 4" x 4'0" long
Shingle lathe	28	1" x 2" x 12'0" long
Shingles		Coverage for 170 sq ft (net)
Ridge cap	2	1" x 6" x 12'0" long
Box stall divider	5	1" x 6" x 6'8" long
Box stall fronts	10	1" x 6" x 2'4" long
Gate posts	2	2" x 4" x 3'9" long
Gate frames	4	1" x 3" x 3'6" long
Gate boards	10	1" x 6" x 1'5" long
Gate cross boards	2	1" x 3" x 3'6" long
Window openings	6	2" x 4" x 2'8" long
Window sill	3	Milled 3'3" long
Window jamb (sides)	6	2" x 6" x 2'1/2" long
Window jamb (tops)	3	2" x 6" x 2'6 1/2" long
Window frame (sides)	6	1" x 4" x 2'3 1/2" long
Window frame (tops)	3	1" x 4" x 2'7 1/2" long
Window sash	3	2'6" wide x 2'0 high, 6 light
Top front door	6	1" x 6" x 2'8" long (trim 30" wide)
Battens	2	1" x 3" x 2'4" long
Brace	1	1" x 3" x 3'4" long
Bottom front door	6	1" x 6" x 3'4" long

Battens	2	1″ x 3″ x 2′4″ long
Brace	1	1″ x 3″ x 4′0″ long
Loft door header	1	2″ x 4″ x 2′8″ long
side frame	2	2″ x 4″ x 3′4″ long
Loft door	5	1″ x 6″ x 3′2″ long
battens	2	1″ x 3″ x 3′0″ long
brace	1	1″ x 3″ x 2′10″ long
Weather boards		1″ x 6″
Front		ca. fifteen 7′2″ long and six 4′8″ long
Back		ca. sixteen 7′2″ long and twelve 4′8″ long
Loft door side		ca. twenty-two ranging 7′8″ to 10′10″ long
Other side		ca. twenty-two ranging 7′8″ to 12′8″ long
Cupola base		4 linear ft per side 1″ x 6″ board
Base frame	4	1″ x 3″ x 2′2″ long
Sides	2	1″ x 3″ x 1′6″ long
	1	1″ x 3″ x 1′7″ long
	8	1/4″ x 1 1/2″ lathe for louvres
Roof frame	4	2″ x 2″ x 1′8″ long
Sheathing	4	Plywood triangles 2′8″ base with 1′8″ sides
Shingles		to cover 9 sq ft net

4. THE BIRD GARDEN

Item	Number	Size/Description
Tree shelves	4	1″ x 6″ x 51/2″ long
Feeding station		
Posts	4	1″ x 4″ x 5′6″ long
	4	1″ x 3″ x 5′6″ long
Platforms	6	1″ x 2″ x 2′6 1/2″ long

	6	1″ x 2″ x 2′5″ long
	10	1″ x 6″ x 2′6 1/2″ long
Roof	4	Triangles of 3/8″ plywood
Thatch or shingles		To cover 12 sq ft net roof area
Bird bath		1′8″ x 1′8″ copper sheet or galvanized metal formed to shape
Bird houses		Builder's choice

5. THE CIRCUS GARDEN

Item	Number	Size/Description
Ring (24′ outer diameter, 9 1/2″ high x 1′0″ wide)	3 3/5 sheets	4′ x 8′, 1/4″ pressure treated plywood
Outer circle	9 pieces	9 1/2″ wide x 8′0″ long
	1 piece	9 1/2″ wide x 3′0″ long
Inner circle	8 pieces	9 1/2″ wide x 8′0″ long
	1 piece	9 1/2″ wide x 5′0″ long
Stakes	110	2″ x 2″ x 2′9″ long
Fill (inside seat; optional)		2 1/4 cu yds of dirt or sand
Top	3 1/2	4′ x 8′ sheets, 1/2″ pressure-treated plywood, cut to fit
Fill for circle		15 cubic yards of sand
Elephant slide		
Body and trunk	4	4′ x 8′ sheets, 3/4″ plywood
Treads	8	3/4″ x 7″ wide, 2′0″ long (from 3/4″ plywood)
Cleats for slide base	2	3/4″ x 1 1/2″ wide x 10′ long (from curves after elephant is cut out from 3/4″ plywood)
Cleats for treads	8	3/4″ x 1 1/2″ wide x 6″ long
Cleats for attaching elephant top to bottom	2	3/4″ x 3″ wide x 6′0″ long

Rosewarne
Learning Centre

Cleats for attaching trunk to head	2	3/4″ x 3″ wide x 1′0″ long
Slide base	1	1/4″ plywood, 2′0″ wide x 10′0″ long
Slide covering	1	Aluminum flashing, 2′0″ wide x 10′0″ long
Canopy		
Legs	4	2″ x 2″ x 3′6″ long
Top frame	2	4″ wide x 2′ 4 1/2″ long (1/4″ plywood)
	2	4″ wide x 2′4″ long (1/4″ plywood)
Top	4	triangles 2′ 61/2″ base, 1′ 11″ sides from 1/4″ plywood
Turtle		
Body sides	2	1″ x 6″ x 1′6″ long
Corners	4	1″ x 6″ x 0′9″ long
Ends	2	1″ x 6″ x 1′0″ long
Bottom (1/2″ plywood)	1	2′0″ wide x 2′6″ long
Top (3/4″ plywood)	1	2′2″ wide x 2′8″ long; corners on bottom and top cut to plan
Legs	4	1″ x 6″ x 1′0″ long cut to shape
Tail	1	1″ x 6″ x 0′6″ long cut to shape
Head	1	1″ x 10″ x 1′0″ long cut to shape
Seesaw		
Main board	1	2″ x 12″ x 10′
Pivot support (3/4″ plywood)		
Ends	2	2 triangles, 2′0″ base, 1′6″ high
Sides	2	12″ wide x 1′9 1/2″ long

For Circus Ring sides:
Allowing for a ⅛" Kerf cut 18, 9½" wide X 8' long pieces from 4 pc, ¼" treated plywood. (There will be one 19⅛" wide piece remaining from the 4ᵗʰ sheet.) Cut one of the 9½" wide pieces to have a piece 3' long and the other 5' long.

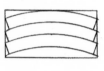

9½" WIDE PIECES

4'

8'

For Circus Ring top:
Cut* from ½" treated plywood sheets 9 arced pieces 1' wide. Note that each arc has a 12' radius. Square off the ends of the pieces along the radius. A 10ᵗʰ piece about 3'3½" long will be needed to complete the circle. This can be obtained from the 19⅛" wide piece left from the 4ᵗʰ sheet of ¼" plywood. Make 2 and double them to get the ½" thickness needed.

For Elephant Slide:
Cut Elephant body from 4 sheets of ¾" plywood as shown. Rotate top sheets to provide for trunk. Slide cleats can then be cut along line of forebody and trunk. Also cut treads and tread cleats from remainder.

*Cut one out and use as pattern for remaining pieces

Counter balance box (optional)

Sides	2	1″ x 12″ x 1′9″ long
Ends	2	1″ x 12″ x 0′9 3/4″ long
Bottom (1/2″ plywood)	1	11 1/4″ wide x 1′9″ long

Cleats (side)	2	1″ x 3″ x 3′2″ long
Cleat (end)	1	1″ x 3″ x 0′11 1/2″ long
Slider bars	2	1″ x 2″ x 6′0″ long
Slider handles	2	1″ x 2″ x 2′6″ long

9. THE PICNIC GARDEN
Picnic Table

Item	Number	Size/Description
Frame legs	4	4″ x 4″ x 2′4″ long
Seat beams	2	2″ x 6″ x 5′2″ long (cut to shape)
Top beams	2	2″ x 4″ x 2′9″ long (cut to shape)
Braces	2	2″ x 2″ x 3′0″ long (cut to shape)
Top	6	2″ x 6″ x 7′0″ long (cut to shape)
Top end cleats	2	2″ x 4″ x 2′9″ long (cut to shape)
Top center cleat	1	2″ x 2″ x 2′9″ long (cut to shape)
Seats	2	2″ x 1′0″ x 7′0″ long (cut to shape)

12. THE ENCHANTED FLOWER GARDEN
The Hansel and Gretel Playhouse

Item	Number	Size/Description
Corner posts	4	4″ x 4″ x 10′0″ long (3′6″ in ground)
Floor beams	2	2″ x 4″ x 8′5″ long
Floor Joists	8	2″ x 4″ x 4′5″ long
Floor	1	4′ x 8′ x 3/4″ thick plywood
	1	1′ x 8′ x 3/4″ thick plywood
	1	1′ x 5′ x 3/4″ thick plywood
Top plates	4	2″ x 4″ x 9′0″ long, mitred on top of corner posts

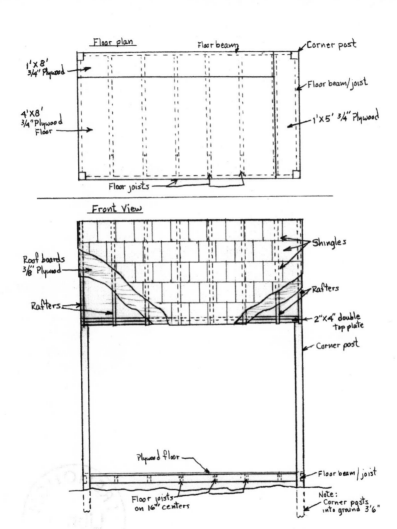

Floor plan

Floor beam

Corner post

1' X 8' 3/4" Plywood

Floor beam / joist

4' X 8' 3/4" Plywood Floor

1' X 5' 3/4" Plywood

Floor joists

Front View

Shingles

Roof boards 3/8" Plywood

Rafters

Rafters

2" X 4" double top plate

Corner post

Plywood floor

Floor beam / joist

Floor joists on 16" centers

Note: Corner posts into ground 3'6"

	4	2″ x 4″ x 5′0″ long, mitred on top of corner posts
Studs (framework)	8	2″ x 4″ x 5′ 10 3/4″ long
Window headers	4	2″ x 4″ x 1′ 4″ long
Door header	1	2″ x 4″ x 2′0″ long
Rafters	16	2″ x 4″ x 4′ 6″ long
Ceiling joists	6	2″ x 4″ x 4′ 5″ long
End boards	2	3′ x 8′ x 1/2″ plywood (cut out for window; cut cutout down center for shutters)
	4	1′ x 8′ x 1/2″ plywood (cut angle to fit gable)
	2	Triangles, 2′11″ base, 2′7″ sides (to fit top of gable)
Back and front boards	2	4′ x 6′ 1/2″ plywood (door cut out of one)
	4	2 1/2′ x 6′ 1/2″ plywood
Roof boards	2	4′ x 8′ 3/8″ plywood
	2	1′ x 4′ 6″ 3/8″ plywood
	2	6′ x 8′ 3/8″ plywood
Shingles		For 81 sq ft net roof area